Father to Son

Ode to Our Black Young

A spoken word celebration
and drum call to duty,
seasoned and spiced
with a gumbo of
new stories

Father to Son

Ode to Our Black Young

Jaiya John

Soul Water Rising

Camarillo, California

Father to Son: Ode to Our Black Young

Printed in the United States of America

Soul Water Rising
Camarillo, California
http://www.soulwater.org

Library of Congress Control Number: 2013923707
ISBN 978-0-9916401-4-0

First Soul Water Rising Edition, Softcover: 2016
Revised printings: 2021, 2024

Poetry / African American / Youth and Family

Editors:	Jacqueline V. Carter Kent W. Mortensen
Cover & Interior Design:	Jaiya John

My enduring gratitude to the African American Advisory Council of the Illinois Department of Children and Family Services, those spirit warriors who insist that our children and families be served sacredly, as fully, divinely human:

Michael Burns
Cretora Barnett
Frances Elbert
Marcia Williams
Joe and Floria Lucas
Diane Cottrell

and so many more
who hold the Light...

When you follow in the path of your father,
you learn to walk like him.

-Ashanti Proverb

We desire to bequest two things
to our children –
the first one is roots;
the other one is wings.

—Sudanese Proverb

AUTHOR'S NOTE

Father to Son, the title poem presented in this book, was written and originally recited as part of a keynote message for the Illinois Department of Children and Family Services *Eighth Annual African American Advisory Council Statewide Conference* in Itasca, Illinois, April 14, 2000. The conference theme that year was a celebration and honoring of African American males, and a call to our collective and personal responsibility. I was honored to deliver my keynote as a last-minute replacement for the poet Nikki Giovanni, she whose spirit in words first broke open poetry in me.

Spirit was a tidal wave with us that day. The audience of around 700 responded to the piece with an energy that I have not experienced since. These wide-open souls were of varied racial, cultural, professional, and personal backgrounds. Each dedicated to honorably serving children and families. They traveled intimately with me through the poetic word flow, exhorting a soulfully charged uprising, a soaked, fervent call-and-response communion reminiscent of traditional African American church praise and worship.

At the last word of the piece, our collective space filled with a resounding silence. Then came a roar, and waves of emotion. This lasted for hours, as we clustered closely in a human circle, not wanting to leave the embrace of Spirit. Men were as teary, dissolved, and physically expressive as were the women. We embraced each other deeply in a moment surreal and persisting.

Something deep inside our generational woundedness and our strength, both as cultural peoples and a societal spirit, had been touched and released. I knew in that moment that these were words for mutual healing.

Father to Son flows out in the context of a people's centuries-old imposed and learned self-rejection, and an ancient, enduring determination to genuinely Love ourselves, Purposefully, no matter. It is a Love letter for anyone who truly cares for the healing and wholeness of all.

May Blessings be upon our dear children, as they journey sacredly into an authentic Love of self, and into an honorable Love for this humanity.

FATHER TO SON

For man who by an ill-borne hand
was ground to dust
shall rise as man again...

The story begins like this:

the father is dying.

his 17-year-old son sits bedside,
near to the fragile form at low tide.

son is reckoning with the greatest terror of his
young life.

they are not alone.

the air is thick and crowded
with the presence of spirits.

harriet is there,
tending to the blisters
on her feet
from all those journeys
on up the road.

sojourner is there,

she carries blisters, too.
hers decorate her skin
and come from the sting of social censorship
as she spoke her truth.

medgar, martin,
malcolm, madiba
—all those who served:

farmer, lewis, parks, abernathy,
nat turner, frederick, booker t,
george washington...
the carver,
biko, bantu steven biko, marcus,
even fannie lou, satchmo too.

all of them are there
splittin' time between private
side conversations
and attending to the matter
at hand:

the dying.

•

evening light sneaking
through the window
is tired but relentless,
like it's ready for bed
but still fixin'
to make a point.

dust dances in that light,
moves its party on over
to the two hands,

the one on the bottom,
frail and covered with
parchment-like
brown skin.

the other, on top,
surging and of skin
supple with nervous sweat.

father and son.
fleeting life,
and young life uncertain.

stillness, recognition, fear.

and then, the father speaks.
these are the words
that will last
for all of time.

he says:

son, for 17 years I've been
trying to find the right words,
the right words to...

what I'm trying to say is—
God, give me strength...

and in that moment, God does.

and the words...
the words are:

Son, I don't know
if you can understand
at such a tender age
what it is that is
truly killing me,
but I have to believe
that one day
light will come from yonder
and grace you with vision.

you have a sister and a mother,
and they desperately need
a brother and a son.

and so you have to understand
that there is a reason
that you and I, Black men,
are the most feared
human beings
on this planet.

the human race
is in a long season
of ignorance.

the ancient lessons
have become a dim vibration

unnoticed by a people tuned
into the wrong frequency.

life has handed down
a circumstance to you
so that you may respond to it
in a way that fulfills
a Divine plan.

never has so much pain
been accumulated
in the heart of a people.

you are an
African American man,
flake of stone hewn
from the mountain
of masterpiece.

•

you have to follow me now, son,
follow me on this.

all the times I told you
that you were lazy,
I meant that I had never seen
so much talent
and it scared me
at what might be lost.

all the times I told you
I Loved you,
what I meant was that I was
in awe of how beautiful
you are to me.

all the times I told you
to grow a thicker skin,
what I meant was
that my heart was breaking
at how this world could treat
something so magnificent
as you like a bacteria
that it simply tolerated
but would be happy
to be rid of.

when I told you to treat
your sister right,
I meant that she needed
your strength to lean on.

when I told you that you don't know
how much your mother needs you,
I meant that Life gave her
a son so that she could look
through you
and see her own beauty as a woman
in ways that other men
could not offer her,

not even myself.

they don't fear you because
you are Black,
they fear you because you represent
men who have always managed to carry
the whole universe on our backs
and *still* stand up straight.

they fear that kind of strength.

they don't fear you because
you're a stereotype of *violence*,
they fear you because
in the way you interact
with other men,
you exhibit a tender,
Loving way that makes their mouths
grow dry in thirst for
the same.

you didn't survive
the slave ship
auction block
plantation pain
family separation
name changes
lynchings
humiliation
whippings
treatment as less than a mule
—God give me strength

you didn't survive
the false accusations of rape

when you were just trying to get home
without having anybody act out their fantasies
of destruction out on you...

the burning glances,
the invisibility (*ralph ellison*),
the physical shackles (*alex haley*),
the psychological chains (*na'im akbar*)...

you didn't survive all of that
to become a generation that
fades away at 17
and becomes a grieving over
what might have been.

•

I didn't raise you like
I needed to,
but no matter how I raised you,
you have the ability to raise yourself
up from whatever circumstance,
because the universe made you *deep.*

the scent on your skin
is a soulful scent,
like burning sandalwood
curling up to the sky that
takes its breath full of you
and then can't help but cry...

because your universe is so very deep.

you can't help that.
you were made
to bring the rain.

they fear your ripeness
because you all are so close
to being a distinctive role model
for all men.

if you can just cross over that Jordan,
if you can just swim through the madness
planted in your mind,
peel back the blindfold
of lies throughout time,
if you can just *see* the majesty within...

•

life handed you pain
because the plan is for you to
become something
with that fertilizer.

you are supposed to become
what centuries from now
will be looked back upon
as a spiritual ascendance
of humanity.

the revolution will not be televised,
cause they can't get no cameras
inside Black boys far enough,

no matter how many ways
they violate them

no cameras that can capture
the sweet soul
of their splendid essence.

this is where the drama
will play itself out,
in the unseen places
where people whose faith lies in the material
tremble with trepidation and cannot follow

because spirit Loves the place
where men are blind.

•

son,
you aren't the trouble,
you're the Light that trouble chases.

you aren't the inferiority,
you are the superiority
that inferior faces.

you aren't the violence,
you're the place violence trespasses.

you aren't the unintelligent,
they only try to miseducate,
uneducate, re-educate you

because they deeply intuit your capacity to
educate the world as to how to truly be a
man.

true soldier,
that's what you need to be, son,
true soldier.

defend your community,
enlighten yourself as to your
constructive *and* destructive potential.

acquire the skills that will allow you
to be a glue
in the community.

true soldier.

resort to violence last,
hold yourself to high standard,
discipline, common cause.

be a shelter
for the younger ones,
be for them what you wish
you had for yourself.

you have withstood the lash
for 400 years,
still they can't get surrender to
flow out with your silent tears.

you have passed enough tests
in this way...
you are qualified to be
a true soldier.

SAT and ACT can't ever qualify you
like enduring
a good old-fashioned
R-A-C   I-S-T.

you, through your people,
have withstood the lash
for 400 years,
the time is now,
let the scar-trees on your back
become maps to a land called
Triumph...
lead us there.

•

father caught his breath,
for he was weak.

he continued:

son,
you have to look around you
and let down your walls
so you can behold
what life has created
as harvest for this earth:

African American men,
which means to say,
men constructed in such a way
as to become the ones endowed
with the responsibility
of carrying the legacy
and integrity
of Africa over to a place
called America
and even through the acid rain
remain the same
soulful, drum beating, dancing,
creating, celebrating, woman honoring,
mother Loving, sister protecting, daughter
cradling, wisdom drinking, peacemaking,
world shaking, Love making, libation pouring,
self-educating, community lubricating,
herbally medicating, physically intimidating,
spiritually mediating, Creator Loving, making
the whole world aching to be like you
but can't admit to wanting
such a thing

so they have to go with fear
and disdain
and create reasons
and programs
and pens and policies
to hold you down
and hold you in
and hold you up

but hold up,
you ain't giving up,
slowing up,
throwing up the African wisdom in you,
the stuff your mama's mama's mama broiled,
baked, boiled, kneaded, basted, fried, ground
down,
snapped, skinned, cleaned, soaked, seasoned,
marinated, created with recipes from memory
and intuition
that called for two teaspoons
of tears and two cups
of passion and pain
and a handful of forgiveness
and just a pinch of desire
and season to taste with:
boy, I'm gon' beat your tail...

all prepared for you to eat from so you could
be full from a meal of our own doing, our own
values, lessons, preachings, proddings,
and other manner of discipline.

no, you were fed
to be belly full,
so you wouldn't have to
go begging
to another culture,
another people's plate
for a meal composed of such ingredients that
your own bowels would disagree violently and
upheave that precious African self-Love
we concocted over eons,

so long before there was an *America.*

you were the ones,
Black boys,
chosen to bring this particular brand
of spirituality
over here to the middle of this
material madness
and yet still emerge after
hundreds of seasons
of degradation
to teach the world a lesson
about how to be men.

you,
Black boys,
Black men,
life chose you to be teachers.

you were given such gifts
in that regard
that all you have to do is
reach into your medicine bags,
pull out the tools of your trade,
and proper class will be in session.

you will teach that violence
is not the endpoint,
nor is it the whole point,
that true men live in harmony with the world
instead of trying to conquer it.

you,
Black teachers,
will teach that science
is not to be the basis
of our spirituality,
but a thread
in our web of knowing

that we choose to believe in things not proven
experimentally,
that we believe in the unseen things:
soul, spirit, vibe, pulse,
funk, rhythm, romance,
ancestors, descendants,
the future, the past,
the dearly departed,
the lives barely started...

the spirits waiting at the door
to be born into seed
between man and woman, waiting for
the flicker of flame to grow into Loving
commitment and dedication
to building a family together
so that the African lesson
can go on being taught

so that we won't have to worry about ever
again being bought,
not with money, material, status,
false power, control...
the sweet seductions of this
candy store place

no, we'd rather believe in
the Spirit,
and Love our Lovers
with a faith in the Spirit

and raise our children
in the company of Spirit

and conduct our communities
to the rhythm of Spirit

not this unnatural cadence,
this out-of-balance drumbeat
given birth by those who never understood
the drum—
our way of talking not only
with each other
but also with our universe.

our whole *being* was packaged
into each beat and sent out
as ripples through the air,
drifting into space,
landing on planets and
bouncing back as sound waves,
to be picked up by the scientific
"creation"
of "*modern*" technology known as satellites,
and *they*...
a hollering and a fussing about how they
discovered evidence of alien intelligence,
all the while denying our African intelligence,

when we were the ones who sent the signals
by drum in the first place.

and they race toward space
as though there is some distant and ancient
civilization out there somewhere

but *we* were that civilization,
not somewhere, but *this* where.

folks more willing to credit martians
than Africans with being intelligent...

see, son, history can be a lie
that conquerors tell.
You want freedom?
Tell your Truth.

•

and why do you think so many *authorities* are
so afraid of you young Black men?

I believe it is because they are representatives
of institutions
whose existence you threaten,
for the equation reads like this:

give a Black man a book
and a reason to read it,
and he turns one key,
cause the reason is all he needed.

give a Black man
a healthy body,
mind, and spirit,
and he turns another key
sure enough,
cause he can't *can*
if he's depleted.

give a Black man
the opportunity
to walk down his intended
road in life
without being hounded
like a dog
and he turns another key.

give a Black man
the space
in which to Love
his Black soul mate,
sister, brother,
daughter, son,
family, friend,
and not be punished for it,
embarrassed by it,
made to feel ashamed for it,
and he will have turned the next key.

give a Black man
a moment to breathe,
so that he may find the universe
inside of him,
and he will have turned

the final key
to unlock the jail house
and set *all* his people
finally free.

•

on the basketball court
they feared michael jordan because
he had fierce excellence within him.

same for jackie robinson,
jack johnson,
and jim brown.

but look, son,
what you have to know
is they fear you
in the school house
that way too.

they fear you excelling
at reading and writing
and science and history,
and most of all,
they fear you excelling
at knowing yourself,
growing yourself,
gaining confidence
in your innate abilities,
because you all were given so much more
than the capacity to play a mean saxophone,

tap dance like a whirlwind, throw
a fierce freestyle rhyme.

you were given things
so much deeper,
such as a natural inclination
to bow down before your elders
and submit to the vastness
of the life *they* have lived.

you
are supposed to show the world
what it means to be there
for your son
when the world tells him
he's a monster.

you give him the tonic
and vision
so he sees his true self:
Everlasting Majesty.

you
are supposed to show the world
what it means to be there
for your daughter...

matter of fact, son,
I want you to do this one day
when you have a daughter:

every month
on the day of her birth,

buy her a rose,
you pick the color

and don't be buying
one of those tired out
supermarket roses either.

go to a flower shop
and buy her
a 10-dollar rose.

you give her that rose
every month
on the day of her birth,
12 days a year
for every year
while she's growing up

and you tell her that
beauty belongs beside beauty
and that's what the rose is for.

that way she will never
ever
be overly impressed
by any wack mack,
slick rick,
smooth groove,
fly daddy
trying to soften her up
with flowers.

she will know
that she deserves
to have beauty
by her side

and that it was
a Black man
who taught her that.

cause a 10-dollar rose
given in the right way
is worth a million

and a rose
given by another game
doesn't truly smell
quite the same.

•

and I want you to do this:

when your mama cries,
you comfort her,
and tell her
it will be all right.

she'll believe in you,
because she'll believe
you have the strength
to take care of her
when she needs it.

make her feel like
she doesn't have to
hold up the sky
all the time

that she can put it down
now and then,
cause you'll be there,
being a man.

•

know something about responsibility.

the community isn't here
to serve you...
you've been given life
so that you can serve
the community.

take the younger brothers
by the hand

look them straight in the eye.

see them.
see them.

teach them about how
you can't be all
you need to be
unless they are all

of what they need to be.

this is called interdependence,
and though our U.S. American
declaration
is of independence,
we African Americans
are not a people
of absolute individualism.

we come from
communal ground.

tell them
you need them to succeed.
tell them
that when they hurt,
you hurt.

use compassion
to color them in,
so they don't walk around
invisible to everyone,
most of all to themselves.

find the courage
to call them out
when they step
in the wrong way.
it might be hard,
but I know
you have
the universe

inside you.

•

and do this:
every time
you get into a relationship
with a Lover,
be a better man
than
you were in the last relationship
with a Lover.

I won't accept you
treading water,
not when you might become
the role model
for the next brother
who steps to
my precious daughter.

make progress.
learn to listen.
tame your ego.
treat them like something special
when you're around people
who are special to you.
understand that half their pain
is about the way this world injures you.

let them feel that pain
with you

and...

•

do this with your son,
because I'm afraid
I haven't done the same
with you:

every time someone
teaches him
that a woman is a
lesser thing,
you hold up life
for a minute
and teach him
the right lesson.

you teach him that
a woman *is* life

that a woman is the passageway
for life

that a woman may
one day
be the light of his life.

•

cry with your son,
laugh with your son,
never *ever* fear your son.

no matter what ugliness
he passes through,
stay there with him,
don't back off.

he needs you
to be the one
to make him hurt a little
so he won't wind up
hurting a lot.

teach him
that a man demands
respect
by demanding of himself
that he *give* respect
to all who cross his path.

that if a man
challenges him
to be a man,
and fight,
that he can only
be a man
if he does not
depend on violence
to gain his sense

of manliness.

teach him
that the poison substances
that carry him
away from his pain
do not truthfully
carry him away
from his pain
but further into it.

teach him
to shout his anger
to the sky

to express
ugly feelings
in beautiful ways

teach him
that this is what
gordon parks
did with his camera,
and robert johnson
did with his strings.

•

teach him
greatness
through humility,
strength

through tenderness,
voice
through silence

and that being hard
is about surrendering
to the softness
of vulnerability.

teach him
to excuse himself
from every table
every time

to nod downward
to people
in respect
and not upward
in dominance

for we were made
to live among
the beauty of Creation
and not above it.

teach him
that the black and white
that people teach us
are always gray
and Grace-filled
when you get down
to the truth of things.

teach him to say please
when he orders his food,
instead of talkin' 'bout:
give me this,
and give me that.

teach him
to keep his eyes off
other people
when he's with
his Lover

and even
when he's *not*
with his Lover.

teach him
that the words
that escape
from his lips
drip with potency
that can either
create or destroy

so he should be careful
and considerate
when he chooses
those words.

•

teach him
to stay on top of
the health of his body,
so he won’t end up
underneath the ground
‘cause he was too busy
gettin’ blazed
or money crazed
or havin’ his sacred song rephrased
into a blues track
for shootin’ smack,
runnin’ game,
sniffin’ fame,
livin’ lame,
eatin’ the same
garbage from the same
self-pollutin’ train.

teach him
that the racism
directed at him
is a compliment
to his potential

because nobody
ever took the time
to hold down something
they thought
could never rise up.

teach him
that the madness
he sees around him
in his community
is not there for him
to emulate
but to eradicate.

encourage him
to tell his story
in as many ways
as possible:

in his clothing
in his walk
in his speech
in the people
he keeps in his life

and through his laughter
and his relationships.

•

teach him
to write poetry
and read books
written by Black geniuses
long before
he ever came along
acting like
he knows everything.

teach him
that before he calls himself
being a man

he better know enough
to recognize that so far
he has only been a boy.

teach him
that when you were a child
you spoke as a child
and understood as a child
and thought as a child

but that when you
became a man,
you put away
childish things.

teach him
that his people need him
to become a teacher in life,
and that to do that he needs
to become a student of life.

teach him
that the reason
it feels so good
to have sex
with a woman
is because you are
rubbing up against
the possibility

of Divine
reproduction

and that *if*
you are not ready
for the baby
then you're probably
not ready
to sex the lady.

teach him
to speak words of
Love and lessons
to his children
in the midst of days
as they pass

not when the days
have run low
and the crossing over
has begun.

people always talking about
how they Love summer
soon as they see
the falling snow.

teach him
to appreciate
the blue in the sky,
the green in the grass,
and the Black in his.... past.

•

ask him
why he thinks he
deserves to be your son.

make him *think*
about the ways in which
he is special to you.

help him to understand
that relationships
are not to be
taken for granted

that they die from neglect,
just like the yard
he never cuts
or pulls the weeds from
or waters,
no matter how many times
you tell him.

tell him
that if he clutters
his relationships with mess
like he does his bedroom,
that a relationship won't
wait around forever
for him to pick up
his dirty drawers.

•

And, son,
remember this
as you continue
to become a man:

Black men must be special,
because why else
would we be given
the tear-inducing glory
of a Black woman
to behold.

why else would we be given
the neck-breaking beauty
in that full ripeness of womanhood...

that nurses us,
comforts us,
stands up for us,
and demands of us
to become all of what we are.

because they see
the universe in us
before we do

I promise it's true.

•

son, the simple truth is:

even in a society
that done gone mad
and calls itself colorblind,
you are undeniably
an African American male.

if you disrespect that fact,
you disrespect the Artist
that painted the portrait
that is *you*
in the first place.

it was Creation Itself
that paused,
took a breath,
looked to the canvas,
and went to the broad strokes
that made you:

bald headed,
dred locked,
fro-ed,
cornrowed,
faded,
slicked,
waved,
redboned,
high yella,
white as night,

coal black,
skillet blonde,
broad nosed,
thick lipped,
honey dipped,
brown eyed,
thick in the backside,
wide from the muscle
made of tussle
with every cotton thorn, scornful glance,
god awful circumstance, indignation,
oil slick,
tar and feather
spit down
from discrimination
and pathological dehumanization.

yeah,
Creator painted you:
chest thumpin',
foot stompin',
voice like barry,
extraordinary visionary.

that's why you're always
makin' up rhymes,
pickin' up sticks,
makin' castles
out of toothpicks.

you soul food Lovin',
hot sauce smackin',
finger lickin',

high steppin',
sensitive brother
masquerading as invincible

but you just a little
greens grubbin',
Lovin' in the bathtubbin',
story tellin',
always tryin' to get over,
comin' crawlin' back like rover,
never learnin',
but still tryin' to get it right

big Black beautiful
kite in flight,
need the wind just right
so you can take off
to your dreams,
get up on a cloud somewhere
and catch a break,
look down on Creation
and realize that
what the Man got
don't look so hot
from up here

that maybe you don't need to
try so hard
to fit in with the mainstream
and accommodate the mainstream
and act like the mainstream
and think like the mainstream

that maybe you already
had your own stream
all along

you just thought the water was
too deep
or too shallow
or too... black.

•

yeah, you got painted
bold and solid
by a Creator gettin' wild
with the brush

thick thighs stretchin' out slacks
made for bony boys

matter of fact,
spendin' life tryin' to fit into other people's
clothes,
other people's schools,
other people's expectations.

you are the circle
stuffed over and over
into the square

but we're all about the circle

and we flow into,

and into
each other
and everything around us.

we are the sweet sunrise
in the breast of bitter morning

the flicker beyond the horizon
the wink of coming light
while still in the clutch
of bitter night.

•

son, ask yourself this
every day:

what makes you
the most feared
human being
on the planet?

you have to be
something powerful
to engender that much fear.

you'll find your own answers
to that question,
but I'm trying to leave you
with mine.

I say
the pain of a woman's childbirth
is beyond men,
because only woman
was meant to be a mother.

I say
the pain of Black boys
and Black men
is beyond other men,
because only we
were meant to show this earth
what it means to rise
from two thousand seasons
of degradation
and shake it off like an
afternoon slumber.

you, my son,
are a Black man,
and you need to know:

you're made from
sturdy lumber.

FINAL LIGHT:

Something in that moment
allowed the words
from the father

to sink into the son.

tears came forth
like maple running in syrup
down bark
not used to bleeding like that.

the spirit of bundini brown
in the corner,
round after round,
exhorting young champion
muhammad ali
to *rumble, young man, rumble!*
slowly built up its presence
within the room.

rumble, young man, rumble!

not a call to violence,
but a demand
that ali let his Black brilliance
shine through the haze
of invisibility and disbelief

that he allow his
Creator-given gifts
to dance and float
and swing and sting
up in that spotlight ring,
and present themselves
to a wounded world,
so all could see
that a man who

releases his blossom
is a beautiful thing.

bundini's voice
started as a whisper so faint,
the son wasn't sure
he had heard it.

it gained volume:

rumble, young man, rumble!

son heard
ali's proclamation
after beating liston:

I shook up the world!

son heard
waves crashing within him,
and he could smell the blatant
scent of salt within the sea.

birds flew over the water
in his mind,
but they were not seagulls,
they were black birds,
Sankofa in flight.

then the drums,
louder, louder...

bundini:
rumble, young man, rumble!

ali:
I shook up the world!

drumbeats

rumble, young man!

I must be the greatest!

drumbeats

rumble!

tears branched out
across high cheekbone

they were their own stream,
they fell from warm face
to cold sheets

young hand grasped
weak hand

strong voice took over:

dad, there's something
I've never told you.

what's that, son?

I've always Loved you.

and I've always Loved myself.
you wanna know why?

why, son?

cause I'll never forget
what you used to tell me
when I was little
and I would come home mad
cause people were calling me
names at school...

telling me to go back to Africa

what was that, son?

you said:

son, tell 'em, *I AM Africa.*
and Africa ain't going
nowhere in me.

and you told me:

don't let that mess
ever get you down,
because you were born
of a Black woman,
of Black ancestral grandmothers,
whose fruit,
like every woman's,

is born *Divine phenomenon.*

•

lifetime of worry
released itself
as subtle smile
on father's face.

weak hand,
father's,
clenched young hand,
son's.

dust finally put down its dance.

light pulled back
to the windowsill.

spirit-folk shook themselves
in awesome wonder,
then got on down the road.

final whisper
from father to son
was both proud approval
and Loving command:

rumble, young man... rumble.

*April 14, 2000

LITTLE BROWN GIRL
WHO WANTS TO WRITE

Whole world wants you
quiet and bowed.
You were born to be bold
and free and proud.

Gotta get your words out.
Gotta say your thing.
Gotta let your truth run wild,
dear child.
Gotta open up
and let your freedom ring.
Gotta stomp.
Gotta dance.
Gotta sing.

Don't be afraid
to let your curls pop.
Your verses drop.
Your sun all the way out.
Your rhythm to roll.
Your soul to stroll.

If you write all the stories
inside you,
you can change the stories
of other little brown girls
just like you.

You can change the world
and help heal the pain.

Or if you want,
you can write just for you.

Your words can be your best friends,
Your playmates,
your own magical worlds.

Write on paper.
Write in the dirt.
Write when you're happy.
Write when you hurt.

Don't worry about writing rules
or being judged by fools.
Write.
Like.
Your.
Words.
Are.
Wild.
Things.

Let them run and hunt
and fly and swim.

Let them dig deep.
Dig your words.

Massage your words
with essential oils.
Burn them like incense,
sacred plants.

Let them Love and laugh
and dream and cry.

Plant them in the soil
to become forests.
Put them in the sky
to become infinity.

Send your words out
to gather all the languages
taken from your people.
And all the lands and waters
and all the memories.

Make your words an offering,
a ceremony,
a Love potion you drink so
you can Love all your ingredients.

Weave your words
into blankets and clothing
and baskets and shelter.

Stew your words into medicine
and feed all living things.

Use your words as candles
and light up the places
you are afraid to go.

Little brown girl.
Get down girl.
Do your thing.

Set yourself free.

Write your words so you can
set flight to your words.

Don't hold them tight.
Burn them bright.
Bless the night.
Bless the day.
Bless your whole life
with your beautiful,
so *you*-tiful,
so incredible,
always edible

words.

*December 1, 2019

OSHUN

The first time . . .
you came chugging toward me
like a coal train around the bend
in purple black night

and I surrendered to you.

Waves, gigantic but laced with kisses,
you crashed against me and took something
of me back with you into your deep other-
place bed.

You whispered, "*Daddy,*" and all my macho
fled.

I pushed tears in heaps out from my eyes,
gathered untapped Love from my heart bed.

I knew it certain, like no other certain before,
I had a baby girl, a daughter, and you were
coming to me, a spirit flying through the
canyons of the spirit world, and you wanted
me, Daddy, a place to nest, and rest and
become your rest.

I've never felt such cotton-soft skin.

You brushed my cheek with yours,
my bristle didn't hurt you, it made you grin.

I've always wondered whether I would be
blessed with that divine human relationship,
to have and to hold children. Now I knew, I...
had a daughter.

You arrived to me like the monsoon,
life-giving, majestic, made me scramble to
start building your throne. Wet, warm, an
overwhelming, oncoming force.

A monsoon, you swept down sky alleys,
filled up long-dry valleys, crossed over the
moon like a rainbow spray of water, calling
yourself to others as my daughter.

You arrived as water.

You arrived to me like the ocean,
endlessly deep, rolling with a thick richness in
your spirit bed, covering everything, holding
all form of Life, wet, warm, ready to feed the
land, to quench all thirst,

you, my daughter, were on your way,
and you called on me that day.

You arrived like ocean,
arrived like monsoon,
arrived a wave towering,
a field flowering,
a brilliant night,
a crystalline day, you filled bays,
combed the tangle of sky-high trees,

shaded the panting forms beneath your flight,
and brought warmth to all shivering in your
sight.

My baby girl, you arrived, out of sight.

You arrived like ocean,
arrived like monsoon,
ocean… monsoon…
oshhhh….
Shoon….

you appeared, you blessed me, you caressed
me, you cried on your daddy's chest,
you filled my daddy breast,
you arrived oshhhh….
like the Nepal rains in June,
you arrived shoon….
like the mariners weeping
on Neptune's bay,

you arrived Oshun.

Oshun, my baby girl, when I'm
spending my daily breaths, I long to hold you.
Wipe the sleep from your deep brown-like-
bambi eyes, carry you over waters wide, dress
you in ancestral song…

My best days are filled with massaging your
little feet, spooning food into your mouth,
wiping the mess from your face, laughing at

your baby grace. All that food all over your
face.

I hold you, sleeping in my arms, watching the
flutter of your eyelids as you dream, blowing
beauty gently into your face, that it might
soak down into those dreams and bring
you happiness.

I run my fingers through your down-feather
hair, pulling straight your tight locks with a
single finger, moving slowly like the deep
stroke of a violin, then letting them beautifully
spring back to kink again.

I change your diapers with a song,
maybe a Love song, maybe a spiritual to take
you back to African dawn.

I clean and powder and clothe that bottom
with a Love that washes me into your
monsoon season.

You grip my finger with your tiny hand, never
letting go, giggling your baby Love into my ear,
I pat your rear.

I burp you in the early morning,
exhausted but giving thanks for this warm
brown angel with your cheek in the crook of
my neck.

I pat you with a steady, warm touch of my
hand on your back and shuuushhh you....
with a melody:

Daddy's here.
You feel me in your baby mind, and think:
Daddy's next to me.

You're my precious spirit child,
something the world has never seen,
and I will prepare a way for you,
kick stones to the side of your road,
pave the ups and downs the best I can,
trusting that you will do the rest,
knowing that your road is not mine to take.

I will write countless poems for you,
sing daily for you, dream for you, walk proud
of you,

I will tell hundreds of stories about my
baby girl to ears that have heard them all
before. And I'll still need more.

We'll blow dandelion seeds on their way,
and feel the tickle of ladybugs on our skin.
I'll teach you to put your ear to the ground
and listen to the grass in conversation.
It will tell you stories of life beneath the
notice of the people world, a life magical
and real regardless of grown folks'
foolishness.

We'll talk about why the sky is blue,
learn to send ourselves to the moon
even when the streetlights go to sleep
and the new sun rises.

I'll pull you from your slumber,
laughing off your sleepy protests to
take you out into the still crisp morning air
and sit and watch The Great Spirit Light
peel off its covers and rise above the horizon.
Sunrise will be our personal, reliable surprise.

We'll walk beside oceans,
our bare feet wet by the embracing sand
and the playful tide.

Side by side we ride beside the tide.

We will talk about pain and what causes
people to hurt one another. We will grow
familiar with fear and uncertainty and hatred
together, so that any storm that may touch
you, you may weather.

We will hold conversation on the oneness of
life, on why people most often do not
recognize this truth,

we will ask questions of the ancestors and
make promises to the future generations.

I will show you how to be in the company of
many even when you are alone.

We will sing in chorus with spirits on our road in our physical solitude,

we will dance and run and swing and jump with our friend, Life.

We will play like instruments flowers, grass, leaves, stones, trees, rocks, water and wind.

We will vibrate our souls through them and they will theirs through us.

I will listen to you, your every breath, pause, word, worry, your every flow of energy, and I will admire and respect your essence and flow. I will go where you go.

And when you go....
a young woman, from the early time in life when Daddy is your shelter tree, into that magical time when you explore the many faces of humanity, I will release my arms with a knowing peace, flush with the recollection that I have given you what I could for your preparation to endure the pains and joys of sexual, sensual, emotional, blossoming womanhood.

I will allow for you a place regarding me whose air carries no thickness from judgment, so that you will easily return to it to lick your wounds and share your gaining treasure cove of memories and meetings.

And the sweetness of your relationships we
shall exalt and never salt your way with
prejudice toward some by virtue of the
wrongs done to you by others.

Our friendship, Oshun, will seek the sky
throughout our passage across seasons, and
we will gain deeper understanding of each
other's souls, even as our bones creak on
creaking porches, and dusk paints
sky and trees with its song of colors.

We together will behold the glory of sundown
and never take for granted the
metamorphosis mighty of steady moon.

And tides.... tides will bring life to your
womanness, your sacred feminine feather,
and both our beds of tears will fall freshly to
replenish our ground,

beholding will we be at the miracles blooming
within your garden of heart and soul vitality.

I will long for your smile like children and
tender souls will long for your touch. Your
spirit will mean that much.

Oshun, our pain and struggle will be sharp
spice that we will use as seasoning for a more
useful stew, and the hurt we at times cause
each other we will use as stepping stones to
strive for higher relationship....

on and on our study of this growth will bring us reward, and the brilliant pinnacle of our Love will be judgment-free acceptance of one another's imperfect being.

In this way we will be intimately bound and fantastically free.

As the cycle high turns back toward its next revolve, my daydreams will grow with brighter resolve to resurrect the original excitement of you, my daughter, Oshun, as you arrived to me.

You arrived to me an ocean,
arrived a monsoon,
arrived a wave towering,
a field flowering,
a brilliant night,
a crystalline day....

And I.... I fed and cleansed, and burped and diapered, and bathed and fussed, and comforted and cooed, and cried and whispered, and swapped smiles, and bossed and worried, and taught and learned,

and beamed and burned, and stood beneath your tidal wave, and parted and returned, and embraced and told stories, and gave warnings in fables and old man recollections of "*when I was your age...*"

and kept from saying *I told you so*, and
watched from afar, and embarrassed from up
close, and tried to be hip, and tempered
my tunes and told never ending daughter
stories, and beheld your relationships and
your growing, and stood beneath your tidal
wave,

and looked deep into pools of spirit in your
eyes, and shared myself and shared myself,
and overcame fears for your sake,

and became

more of a soul for you, more of a medicine
for you, more of a child-like joy for you,
more of a healed and peaceful place,

a sturdy tree, a shaded spot, a warming
blanket, a cooling breeze,
a wise source, an understanding ear,
a responsive caretaker, a freeing
authority, an inspiration, positive sensation,
reliable vibration,

a deep well for dipping, a ladder for reaching,
a light ray for the breaching,
a compliment to your needs, a recognition of
your strengths, a passive admiration,
an active education, a chant, a prayer, a
resting chair, a shelter, a path, a drink,
a calming, clarifying, connecting, parallel,
easy, relaxing, humorous, challenging,

humble, Loving, ever-and always-lasting place to come home.

And that is how you will arrive to me.

Like you arrived to me then.

As I.... stood beneath your tidal wave

Oshun.

*Oshun: *An African goddess. The River Goddess of Sweet Water and Beauty.*

*Spirit brought these words through me one year and four months before my daughter was born. Seven months before she was conceived.

March, 1997

NILE RIVER WOMAN

600 BC…
and her brown hands
pull the mud from its bed of earth, working
purposefully in the cool of morning.

She works at a whisper,
trying not to wake the sun
dozing behind the ridge
but already stretching its fingers
through the green braids and dreads
and afros of the river trees.

Her hands are much like the Nile mud
she pulls, caked and lined,
skin thick and tracked with stories.

Even in this early air,
a bead of moisture meant for cooling springs
from a forehead pore,
gathers itself for a moment,
then drops on a journey,
long and free as drop journeys go,
finally landing on the mud
her hands are now massaging.

Her cooling drop mixes
with the mud's river moisture,
moisture stewed with insect shells,
animal hairs, strands of tree moss,
algae colonies orphaned
from their rocks.

She brings the mud to clay
by Loving it with hands
that are wise at Love,
squeezing, pushing,
reassuring the mass,
like she has her men before.

The thrusts of many Lovers
has pounded flat
the small of her back,
and endless loads of sticks,
of water, and of grain
have rounded her upper back
closer to the earth,
but she squats with a confident sturdiness,
her leathered feet sunken
four inches into the wet,
giving mud,
covered itself with a thin layer
of the river's shoreline breadth.

The lick of the water
against her ankles is pleasurable
and the wetness creeping
slightly up her cloth wrap
and around her rump
reminds her of long ago arousal.

She works the clay
until it fulfills her vision
of a rounded pot
with puckered lip,
then lets it mature

beneath the play
of the now-frisky Sun.

She will use the pot
to cup her sister's milk.
Sucking on the sibling nipple,
she will transport the sweet milk
from her cheeks to the pot
with a low pressure spray
from her lips.

This milk will be used
for her sister's baby,
and the twin babies
of the village woman
whose own breasts bring no milk.

She will also use the pot
to gather river water
to cool her daughter's baby
when a fever brought
from a sour wind
threatens the infant's life.

She will use the pot
to catch the goat's blood,
sprayed out in a delicate stream
from a small, precise incision.
This will be for the ceremonial
drinking when the moon
reaches its peak swell
before birthing
the next litter of stars.

She will leave countless tracks
in the riverside mud
that gave birth to this pot
as she returns to and from the water,
sometimes gathering plants
to grind into paste
in the bowels of the pot
to salve wounds,
to calm angry stomachs,
or to ease the sting of mosquitoes.

And yes, at times the paste
will be Love potion
for the use of young
and older women weary
of coaxing passion
from those they desire.

Sometimes, though,
she simply visits the river
to gather the water into the pot
for cooking or drinking,
or for treating lengths
of leather rope.

Over the course of her remaining life, during
the many times
she will have held the pot,
the shadows of clouds and dragonflies and
vultures and fire smoke will have stolen
repeatedly across her back,
the durable Loving
between pot and hands

will have imparted the woman's
finest palm lines into the grain
of the pot in permanence.

And when she finally walks
back down into the earth
for Eternity,
the pot's final task
will have been to cradle
the ashes of the physical proof
of her being.

PRESENT DAY....

The pot, now centuries-wise
but currently at rest,
sits amongst a collection
in a cultured man's home,
and a visitor remarks:

That's an incredible piece
of intact pottery.
That should be in a museum.
Where is it from?

And the cultured man,
proud, proclaims:
It's from the Nile,
circa 800 BC.
The person who made that
made it to carry water.

And the Spirit world's
whispered response:

She made it for much more than that.

*October 19, 1995

WHY WE GOT THE BLUES

Brother gotta
gotta go
gotta get some quick
gotta put flame to his candlestick
gotta feel good 'cause things
got him down
gotta talk smack
whack sister friend on her
booty back pack

Brother gotta put lips
on some weed
gotta puff haze between
his truth and his need
Brother gotta ride video joystick
'til fingers bleed
got confidence in those skills
Naw, aint gonna pay no bills
but got some mad joystick skills

Brother gotta get outta bed
this Saturday night
gotta breathe the air outside
gotta find hip-hop scene
gotta move heels to the beat
gotta feel good sometime

Brother gotta fill his pockets
got lil' brother man to feed
got male ego to pay heed
got Mama to pay back

for all her heartbeats lent
time Brother laid out drunk
in the street
time Brother beat a steady retreat
from the books
from the dinner table
from callin' his father Pops
Naw, still aint given Ma her props

Brother gotta
gotta get some peace
gotta take that art class
gotta pay out that lease
least before he gets a cool,
mellow, barley-hop,
peace pipe pop on
gotta coach lil' nephew man's
Little League baseball crew
got six innings to do

Gotta check out that chest pain
jumpin' up with every drop of
American rain
gotta get the stains out his jeans
gotta come correct to Baby's porch
gotta light her torch
gotta feel good sometime

Brother gotta
gotta go
can't spend his whole life
shovelin' other people's snow
gotta clear his own path

gotta drain baby daughter's bath
water got cold, needs fillin' up

Gotta check those tears
got fears, gotta stomp 'em out
got posse, got crew,
gotta keep his clout
Yeah, Brother got juice,
don't squeeze him none
putrid mess will run
Damn, gotta get that gun

Gotta cut that hair,
gotta fit the company image
Image don't take no 'fros, no fades,
boxes, braids, Marley locs, no flattops
Naw, gotta be good like Goldilocks
gotta check his diction
Brother flow aint gonna work
gonna be their fiction
when they want some fact
like some Shakespeare-style
quackedy-quack

Brother gotta
gotta choke that deep fried
hurtin' back
seen lil' sis' sent up the Mississip
lookin' for a good man
seen Mama prospectin' for gold
with a fryin' pan
Lookit all the complaints
in the lines of her hands

Brother gotta
gotta creep, gotta find somethin'
tasteful in the night
gotta wash down the grit with some
kinda segregation turpentine
gotta kill off the nerve synapses
'fore sleep comes a callin'
aint down for no more dreams
about this Brother fallin'

Gotta hoof it to work
ride got in a wreck
gotta get that next paycheck
Aw, heck
that aint enough,
gotta get somethin' quick
can't crime no more though
gotta start shovelin' his own snow
Man, Woman,
Brother gotta
gotta go

Gotta go out and look up at the stars
gotta feed his dog
gotta get some body oil
for his Baby-woman
gotta get some bubble bath
for his Baby-child
gotta find some answers in the dark
really gotta swallow the fear
and the frowns
the hate and the lack of faith he gets
in the stores, from passing cars,

on the streets, in elevators, hospitals,
courtrooms, classrooms, homes, offices,
from government, landlords, librarians,
liberals,
gotta swallow it all
and spit it out his
mouth

Gotta get South
explore his roots,
gotta chew some roots
drink some herbal tea
gotta heal his insides
gotta get free

Brother gotta kneel
in the sunrise mist
take a pause for his flaws
take a breath for his thanks
drop a tear for the days
he has lived
grab some dirt
spread it on his face
mark his value
as part of the human race

Wish Brother could sit a spell
and drink a glass of ice-cold peace
but Brother gotta
gotta go
Gotta feel good sometime.

*January 6, 1996

COMFORT OF A RHYTHM

Wipin' sleep from my eyes
kickin' sheets off my feet
Swingin' feet to the floor
can't sleep no more

Wipe sunlight off my face
rub down my stiffed-up knees
Givin' thanks for another day
finishin' prayer with a please

Hear dogs claimin' territory
fendin' off fools from the fence
Barkin' for sexual drive
soundin' off just to act alive

Kickin' brother in the head
him still snorin' plus he
bothered me all night with
his cold feet
Got reasons to feel
some kinda way
on this butter meltin day

Smell some kinda somethin'
fryin' in the pan
don't notice the heavy footsteps
in the house from the old man

Hear the faint tick... tick
out on the porch
Feel kissin' on my neck from the

clean country breeze
tick... tick...
Mother pickin' stones
from black-eyed peas

Cinch up my drawers
pull on my trous'
Rub on my belly
Stand to stretch my spine

Reassert my presence in the house
as I go into the kitchen
Met with a nod from Uncle
a pat from Lil' Man
nothin' from Sis'
pure dismiss
but I get "Mornin' Honey,"
from Ma's twin sister,
my aunt, Chaalis

Pour water thinned milk
in my cereal bowl
look out at the trees
faint tick... tick
Mother pickin' stones
from black-eyed peas

she says, "Pouchy and Rick said
meet 'em down my the crick."

Take out the trash, kick brother
in the head for good measure
grab my outdoor hoopin' ball

spread some shea butter
on my dome
"Smooth like that..."
head out to where I can feel good
no eyes 'pon me, no doubts
no American Black man bouts

Pause on the porch
Promise chores to Ma
rub her head real quick
with my fingertips
hit the dusty road,
pursing sweet mornin'
between my lips

Turnin' the bend outta sight
catch myself smiling to the
faint tick... tick in the breeze
Mother pickin' stones
from Black-eyed peas.

*January 9, 1996

I'VE GOT TUBMAN FOR A RIB BONE

My name is Humanity,
and I've got a story to tell.
Last night I had a conversation
with Inhumanity,
and the flow
went something like this:

Inhumanity spoke:

Humanity,
I can't figure you out, man.
I keep slapping you down,
but you don't, you won't,
stay down.

I've taken you in chains
from your land and your family,
packed you like spoons
in dark floating coffins for weeks,
branded you,
humiliated you on trading blocks, whipped
you, renamed you,
sold you, strung you up,
beat you down,
raped you, castrated you,
tar-and-feathered you,
labeled you three-fifths human,
tore apart your families,
took your religions, languages,
customs and beliefs,
segregated you,

caused division amongst you, incarcerated
you,
made you think like me,
made you want to look like me,
shaped you in my image.
I did all this to you,
and still you won't stay down.
What's up with you, Man?"

And I, being Humanity, answered:

But you don't know me though.
Check this out.

I've got Harriet Tubman
for a rib bone.
You think you can sucker punch me
and win the fight?
I can take your body blows
like Ali all through the night.

I will never lose
because Tubman never lost
a single slave.
She retired undefeated.
Undefeated.
Are you feeling me?

I've also got Sojourner Truth
for a heart.
That means I will travel endlessly
to fulfill the Truth of me.

Frederick Douglass is my mind,
a fierce Lion that will struggle
to the death for progress
toward what I know is mine.

Steve Biko is my backbone.
I will never bow down to you
from fear.

My tongue is Alex Haley.
I will always tell stories of my Roots.
You hear?

Rigoberta Menchú is my ego.
I will forever retain my humility
and never think of myself
as being better than my people.
The material will not seduce me.
My feet will root in the Earth.

Martin is my dreams.
My vision is clear and far
as I stand on the mountaintop,
my feet wading
in righteous streams.

My endurance is Frida Kahlo.
You will not break me,
even as my body breaks.
I will splash this world
in the bold colors and visions
of ferocious freedom.

My spirit is Cécile Fatiman.
Like an ancestral sapling
I will rise and I will rise
and birth fresh forever forests
of revolution and reclamation.
I will birth freedom's nation.

And dig this,
my blood is El-Hajj Malik El-Shabazz.
You may know him as Malcolm.
My scarlet flow runs hot,
never allowing me to be cooled
by your token pacification.

My eyes are Gordon Parks.
I see through your agenda
to the harsh reality
of your poisoned soul.
I will capture the medicine
of my people's beauty
in images you can never erase.

My dignity is Rosa Parks.
I will NEVER accept
living less than first class
or less than fully human.

I said all this
and Inhumanity quaked in its shoes.
But I wasn't done.

I said:

You slew El-Shabazz at 39.
You slew Martin at 39.
You slew Biko at 30.
You slew countless others
In the shadows beyond
public notice.

You thought you could kill me off
young.
But I rose up, again and again,
stronger every time.
This is because I am the Body Human,
unconquerable blossom
of the Spirit of Life.

Inhumanity now was crying,
on its knees and small.
It was wobbling, wavering,
ready for the final knockout blow.

I obliged.
I said:

Here I am again before you,
in my current form and life.
Slay me to the ground this time
and I will come stronger yet again,
rising higher than a kite.
Inhumanity, you better recognize.
I am Humanity,

and I've got Tubman for a rib bone.
You will never, EVER, win this fight.

And then... I turned out the light.

*November 19, 1997

THE COTTON FIELD

Rows
and rows
of Negroes
in afros
and cornrows
elbows to elbows
dragging pick hoes
in the throes
of who knows

but I suppose
they knows
cotton always grows
and there ain't no chance
for winter snows
no hurricane blows
to pause their woes
or the bloody footprints
they sows

so they just keep on
singing from
heads to toes

carry they blows
on backs scarred
with tracks
like broken arrows
wishing they was
arapahos
or seminoles

anything but
whiplashed negroes

and there ain't
no no-shows
they all keep standing
as the sun blazes
and steals life
from they bone
marrows
they eyes narrows

sweat falls from
burnt skin
like nervous sparrows
'cause if one falls
they all fall like
rows and rows
of dominoes

one does fall
but he quick to rose

he rose (heroes)

then another fell
but she quick to rose

she rose (sheroes)

sheroes
and heroes

Rows
and rows
of Negroes
in afros
and cornrows
elbows to elbows
dragging pick hoes
in the throes
of who knows
but I suppose
they knows

they knows
they live
for their
children's better
tomorrows

they knows
they lows
are for so's
you and I
can live like

we suppose'

God bless
them beautiful Negroes.

*June 14, 2001

SOMEONE AMONG US

Now fire that's a thing
that burns from the inside out...

freedom from what?
freedom to what?

Some one among us brung us
Some one among us stung us
Some one among us
done hung us!

Humungous fungus
done come among us

Blood cells took sickle shapes
that colluded to
stick and stumble
earth beneath us
startin to cumble

and she she got the sugar
poor little booger
and he he got the spells
and he he prostrate growing
like prize winnin' pumpkin
in the monsoon season
and she skin flakin like
bleached sea shells
we got the dermatitis
the colitis
the arthritis

the gingivitis
Lord help us
come right us

Children come soon
and see your pa
he got the chicken bone
stuck in his craw
He got the vertigo
walkin like see-saw
see he saw what was comin
started bumming and hummin
way back tunes
down by the river
and over Jordan and such
he got himself spiritual crutch
took to song
won't be too long
he got the chicken bone
stuck in his craw
children come soon
come see your pa

Carter G. see
Carter we

talkin' 'bout 'you meet 'im,
you meet 'im?"
Boy how'd you defeat Freedom?

I got between 'em
and kneed 'em

you gotta deceive ‘em
to bleed ‘em

here we are
sole remainders on the ark
all around us the flood
can’t drift forever
we find ground or drown
who’s gonna be the healer
the teacher
who’s gonna be the prophet
who’s gonna be the preacher
who’s gonna be the Lover
the leader
who’s gonna be the soldier
the seeker

who’s gonna look the child
in the eye
who’s gonna live life half-steppin
while his soul shrivel up and die
who’s gonna man the oars
who’s gonna steer the rudder
who’s gonna stop the seepage
who’s gonna calm mama
when she shudder
got two cows
and two sheep
but two of those four
done gone empty in the udder

who’s gonna make milk
for the babies

who’s gonna diagnose the illness
when the whole boat get rabies
who’s gonna take action
and stop runnin’ at the mouth
with the maybes

all around us the flood
and everybody got a bucket
but some too weak to lift it
everybody got gold in their
prospecting pan
but some too tired to sift it
everybody got a song to sing
but some too scared to riff it

who’s gonna love like Jesus
and walk like Jesus
and Jesus believe us
we got troubles, receive us
relieve us, reprieve us,
weave us, from dust
to rock to rain to light
please...
we need us

new land ahead
where no one can bleed us
gotta get there though
so who among us
ain’t gonna be the one
who stung us
who got the bones
to not forsake us

who got the Love
to feed us
the medicine
our children will say
that there freed us

oh Lord
we need us
oh Lord
we need us.

*October 10, 2002

SIPPIN SWEET TEA

SIPPING sweet tea
from preserve jars
in the silent moment
'tween daylight and stars

summer sweat
slick on tanned skin

Jeremiah perched on porch stairs
pickin' sweet tunes on six strings

cicadas dig the groove
sayin' hey from the cypress trees

cool breeze
condensation
slidin' down the glass

cubes melting real slow
in the sugar bath
children chasing butterflies
on down the path

tall grass holding garter snakes
and croakin' toads
this is just one of those moments
in one of those days

upstairs kneeling next to bed
Big Ma prays and sings
hands holding the old quilt
fresh from the hangin' line

uncle Terry loose
on his cheap wine
passed out on the deep end
of his shallow dreams
he's climbing sky high
summer vines

antique clock keeps on
keeping stock of time
like each tick
is a brick of wishin' gold

carpet's wore bare
from Big Ma's wheelchair
and summer parties by the dozens
so we don't care

memories of laughter
and jukebox flirting
dance in the passion
settled on the window skirting

windowsill dust remembers
candles burned down
and bobby pins left behind

oven's broke but still bakin'
some *baaad* pound cake
in the morning
she burns catfish and eggs

hound dog out back
on three legs
still chasing rabbits
and shadows down by the creek

down where the young ones
skip their stones
and Lonise lost her innocence
in tender moans

hot combs on the porch
and pomade on the rail
let you know who's
getting her 'do did
and who's
fixin' to shake her tail

hot lips on the cool glass
take down that last
sweet tea swallow

empty drinkin' jar catches
first drop of rain

it's just one of those days...

*July 25, 2006

BLACK MOSES

You think Harriet's back ached?
you know her feet were blistered
past all appeal

mud musta grabbed her
almost up to the knees

whenever it could get a hold of her
she moved like breeze

her dark skin musta worn
a mud cloth coating
'round the legs up to her seat
mud heavy and tight
in the mosquito heat

speaking of which
she musta been feasted on
'squitos love the thick glow
of defiant soul

she musta had a wonderful humor
we don't know about
how else you gonna lead folks
up the river with dogs
at their back
and they ain't even sure
they wanted to go

she musta cracked on everything
she could wrap her
mind around just to get a laugh
from the clench-jawed
males trying hard to be men

or to calm the babies
and courage up the grown ups

I bet her laugh
was a full throated cackle
bet she rousted the moon
that's why it faithfully shone
its eerie light
on their path as a boon

you gotta figure
she cried when the others
weren't watching
some for their pain
some for their grieving
some for what she knew
they had coming if caught

her tears woulda been too salty
for the pretty flowers
they trampled on their way
too sweet for the pondweed
they passed by the day

most of the time
she had to have been
choking back fear
telling herself
I gotta hide gotta hide
woulda been speaking
of her tempest inside

she knew if they were caught
white savagery would have
washed their black
in deep red

and the children
would have to step numb
over the countless dead

her eyes musta been
watery floating in worry
her breath shoulda stank
cause those things
don't matter much then

her scalp caked in sweat
her hair matted down
beneath that soiled scarf
as a crown

her knees had to be creakin
her bursa sacs leakin
blood pressure pressin
her dogs barkin and speakin

her hands probably knotted
around whatever they carried
rifles and stones
and children and figs

she woulda come to know trees
'long the way
and river bends
and surely amens
at the end of the pray

she musta ate poorly
and digested it worse
guts all tied up snakes
trying to get loose

you know her ears
heard slave catchers cursing
when it was only
the northeastern leaves
steady rehearsing

surely day played cruel games
on her till dusk
she couldn't bathe none
she must have smelled
all of musk

prone to sleep fits
by exhaustion or worse
and burnt by the sun
she was a dream walking
delirious ex-slave on the run

you can imagine her
daydreaming about the drifting
white cloud directly above
wishing she could hitch a ride
on that unbridled
black bird

So now when they say
ol' Harriet she led her people
to freedom
they haven't said half the word.

*August 31, 2006

I WAS AFRICA ONCE

I was Africa once
before the nets and ropes
and shackles and spit
and spite that clouded
my vision of self

I was Africa
and not nearly perfect
but undistorted
rooted
and fully human

I was Africa
under the banana leaves
dripping with clean rain
civilized more then than
after civilization came for us

I was stronger than
the rotting log
teeming with decay
weaker than the granite stone
whitening in the salt of bay

I was Blackfeet
in the heat
of genocide
Cherokee too
and not because
it was a foolish fad
I was born from that tree

born for my clan naturally

I was the blisters
on young hands
learning Old Father's
deeply oiled drum

I was the eternal hum
in Buddha's throat
before foreign power
came to our temple
to prey

I was Christ's true intent
before ill spirits twisted Love
and compassion
into words for weakness

I was the slave
lying still as death
just beneath water's surface
my back joined with the mud
waiting as lungs exploded
for the catchers to pass
praying for their dogs
to miss my scent

I was Blackfeet
holding elder council
on cold wide plains
our social wisdom
was ocean-deep
and yet we *succumbed*

they said
because we were not
ambitious enough
to become capable of
owning our land

I was Seminole
spraining ankles
to get through swamp
to our desperate home
the catcher's couldn't bear
so we built a new world
in our brutal mangrove lair

within that blistering heat
and mosquito cloud
least we had a chance
to be left alone
and left alive

I was sure I was human
I was clear I was beautiful
I was known. I was seen. I was home.

I was all of that
before I was this

I am Africa
I am Indigenous
still.

*October 29, 2006

GRAMA'S SONG

It's not that I didn't like it
when Grama set on the porch,
rocking in her chair,
singing that song
as the sun went down.

It's just that I got with jealousy
the way she led the Blackbirds
to hold up their own song
and take audience with her.

I didn't cotton to the silence
that crept from the innards
of the forest which stood guard
around the beaten yard
surrounding our house.

And I didn't cotton to the silence
that crept from the trees
and held our house in its gaze
as Grama set a'singing
in her glorious haze.

"Sit a spell," she would say,
and all the momentum of the day,
all the progress I had made
toward being a normal child,
would come abruptly
to a shuddering end
as Grama courted the woods

with mighty lungs
and seductive air.

The creaking of her rocking chair
provided an earthly
background pulse and cadence
to her supernatural wail.

Together, the sounds drifted up
into the sky
and toward the treetops
like wafts of steam
from a stack of golden flapjacks.
And indeed, just like those flapjacks, leading a
child from slumber,
Grama's voice would call forth
the woods.

When I was young,
like I was when Grama
sang from the porch,
I yearned to blend into
my surroundings
'cause I was shy
and of humble ways.

I did not think it proper
to call a thing
so Mighty and Old
and Deep as the Forest
to attention—the attention
that was so total and loyal
as that when Grama sang.

The sky would grow orange
and a cooler air
would begin to settle in
amongst the warm air,
telling of its intention to nestle comfortably
into the bed of night.

Some nights I swear
I could actually hear
the animals out there
scurrying to settle
their daily business
so's they could be ready
to catch Grama's show.

"...the bones, they grow...
silent and upright,

like cornstalks in the night...

...the bones, they grow...
silent and upright,

like cornstalks in the night..."

She would sing this,
and the words were soaked
with *Ebony* and *Wisdom*.
Ebony and *Wisdom*...
the sky seemed to drink
these things like fluid
down into its gut,

and I guess that explains why
every couple of weeks
the sky would grow too heavy
and have to give up its load.

A thick, Black rain
would pour down
in bursts and sheets.
We all—my Grama,
brothers and sisters and me—
we would sense when the sky
was about to cry,
and we would go quick
and stand out on the porch.

Outside in the deepening orange
and cool air eager for bed,
the *Ebony* and *Wisdom*
filled our world
and soaked us.

Coated and choked us.

Rose at our ankles
and dripped from our chins.

Saturated our hair
like water in a sponge.

And then it was done.

The effect of all this
was something you may take

pain to believe.
Nohow, truth is,
this cycle—Grama's song,
and the showers
of *Ebony* and *Wisdom*—
was the self-same thing
which kept us Black and Wise.

Grama's Grama told her so,
and then Grama told us too.
Now I'm telling you.

It's not that I didn't like it
when Grama set on the porch,
singing that song.
It's just that I was
a child at the time,
and straight frightened with awe.
You can't believe the things...
the craze...the madness I saw.

It's many years since now,
and I'm a child no more.
But some nights
when the air is still
I can just about believe
I'm hearing the bones
growing silent
in the cornfields,
and I wish for Grama's thick,
giving arms around the part of me
that is a child still.

Grama passed on
some time ago,
but I know there must be
someone else's Grama
out there singing her song,
'cause I'm still Black and Wise,
and I'm still going strong.

*January 27, 1995

SHEBA

Glorious mothers and sisters
wives and daughters
laboring souls crowned
with evidence of striving
enterprise rising

blossoming of families
spice-seasoned moments
of spirit-rich days
Smelling like tropical breezes
in your queenly stroll through life

Whispering hints of coconut oil
chocolate and lilacs
through the breath of your pores

You are Sheba
the scent of woman
stately towers of resilience
in wandering winds
cascading sheets of golden fabric
free-flowing threads
blowing in elegance
around your body
heralding the freedom
with which you flow
displaying like sunset
the aural ripening
of your female glow

You are Sheba
exuding your unique smile
through folds and blends
of African dress
exalting your heart
through splashes of every color
through vibrant patterns
of quilted commonality
commonality that you Sheba share
with Woman Indigenous
with Woman Africa Asia Arabia Europa
with tides of Woman washed up in
companionship on every shore

You are Woman and more

Sheba the peacemaker
to you we turn for our final peace

Sheba the warrior
your Love fights our battle
with domination in the least

Sheba the soul wading by the river gathering
cool water in your palms
to cleanse the child
to refresh the spirit
to feed the land

Caking radiant riverside mud
smoothly across your cheekbones
you are painted beauty
searching for a throne

Shaking down autumn leaves
from a final treetop slumber
you dance with a woman's hips
a woman's legs
you dance an enchanting number

Upon that brown and orange
autumn leaf-swept floor
you dance the dance of creation
of healing
you dance for more

Captivating robes and turbans
towering high
maroon blushes
accessory jewels
hanging from the Sheba tree
you are scent and storm
and calming sea

Sheba you are the hands
of Woman joined across
the great expanse
in your grasp lies our earthly bond
and warmth-fed hope
Sheba
you are the Freedom Rope

You gather all by the fires
settling the elderly
over by the sheltering tree
bringing the children close
by your knee

You gather the men closest
to the warmth of the flame
for you know a proper Sheba fire
will bring their restless souls
some at long last tame

You gather all by the fires
in the dimming daytime light
and rising up on the wisps of smoke
you, Sheba, grab the night

You say:

Walk tall the aged
for your feet have calmed the path

Walk tall the youthful
for this blessed path next is yours

Walk tall the Men of men
for you must help
to cleanse our sores

Walk tall the weary
for rest soon shall come

And walk tall the fallen
there is LIFE left to rise up for

Strokes of cosmetic kiss
across my face
the mist of garden fragrance
around my form

endless flowing scarves
and cloth like ribbons
of waterfall
caressing from shoulders high
on down to earth
powerful tones and hues
and simple truths
in color and cloth
shout out my mirth
For I am Sheba
I am every glorious woman
and with you all as companion

I shall walk tall upon this Earth.

*April 26, 1995

SISTER STEW

Crisply,
the turning of the seasons,
annual blossoming of leaves
from greens to golds
and scarlet folds,

drops of maple on fallen leaves
sweetly tinge the air
as the burning of tree-fall
splashes life in streaks
of seasonhood.

Warmly,
the turning of the healer's hands...
massaging over healing lands,
and floral scents fill the vacuum
of inner space
as human touch human,
and emptiness is erased.

She fills she
with spoonfuls of her
Love and affection,
and recipient sister-friend
becomes a recipe for blossoming,
becomes a deep-fry batter
for spirit-rising
to shame even the ripest yeast.

She fills she,
and their joining
caresses the trespass of the seasons.

Yams, squash and plantain crop
glow a color dance
to partner with the turning
of the leaves
and fill bellies,
to soothe heartbreak,
to swell the tides of joy,
to tenderize the figs of recollection,
to capture fleeting mother-moments inside
their sweetened skin,
like children chomping apples and dripping
juices from their grin.

And friendship grows like this,
a skyward pulsing
of the Autumn drums
to faithfully remind friend of friend, remind
she of pain and pleasure,
remind she of memory
and of spirit treasure.

The drumming a harvest rain
pitter-patter,
and crops grows fatter,
vibrations through chest
of ancestor drumming,
each vibration the sound
of sister chord strumming...

All the while
October dusk shadows creep over
woman vibration,
intuition and vision,
painting dark gray canvas
over sister magic,
leaving she and she
as centerpiece
in floral masterpiece,

honey-sweet capsules of lilac
and morning glory-kiss
break free upon blossoming
and take to the air,
a lavender spray of sister mist.

Chocolate beauty flows as lilac grows,
for sister river irrigates the flower bed.
Healing hands gain seasons
and through wisdom's circle
to soul mate are wed.

Each twelve moons become sweeter
for she and she,
for falling leaves
make ground richer,
and strengthen the earthy root.

She fills up she,
and leaves fall to the ground.
Ground becomes island stew.

Special ingredient:

The oneness of two
a lifetime through.

*October 7, 1997

HARVEST

In the name of my father's father, who was my flesh in the fading dusk of slavery day, I spirit-walk to his side and listen for what he has to say.

And in my walking, I am sent to a place where the mist spray of morning tide in caress of Ghanaian coast coats me, a cold shower of recollection.

As Autumn moon splashes down into Winter cocoon, I am enraptured by dual voices, the past and present, drumbeats in syncopated cadence, calling to me.

I hear their voices as mist and whisper, and they dance a lesson into my ear. They are familiar, they are near. They are ancestral, so I pause to hear.

As mist and whisper I do hear. I hear:

Go back, go way back. Go back and clean yourself in the Earth. Go back and back. Go back and back. Go back and get Black in that rich coffee Earth. Let nitrate and sulfate and phosphate invade your pores and send you to distant shores. Go back and get Black, back to the time when we were community. Then, bring it back.

Prepare the ground, turn it over, make it fertile with decomposition so that it may bring forth a symphony composition of nutrition and plenitude.

Prepare the ground, prepare the family for the coming of child. Prepare the ground, prepare the family.

Plant the seed in black earth, plant deep or shallow as necessary, but let the seeds drop with Love and delicacy from your fingers into their black soil bed, so that Nature's fate will treat the seed with same Love and delicacy.

Plant the seed in black earth, plant the seed in womanhood. Plant the seed in black earth, in womanhood.

Water the ground, tend to the sprout. Irrigate and separate weed from intended seed. Ask for the rains to fall, watch them bleed. Bleed life into your seed.

Water the ground, tend to the sprout. Care for the pregnancy, prepare a home, pass the word. Gather resources and consider the Spirit to come.

Water the ground, tend to the sprout. Beat the drum. A Spirit come.

Follow the moon, for it is shy. It will peek behind darkness most nights in the sky. But when it comes full for the ninth time, watch for the ripeness, feel for the firmness. Greens will turn to red and yellow, or simply a darker green. And corn will begin to whisper, husks brushing against one another in the wind.

Begin.

Harvest. Birth. New Life. To sustain life. A reason to celebrate. And if you believe in a Higher Power, then you have the most reason to celebrate, because you know that the providing comes from Above.

You have raised the crops, now raise the children. Harvest season.

Husk the corn, clean the children. Shell the nuts, settle disputes in the compound. Snap the beans, child, help your Amma snap the beans.

Sift the grain, get the pebbles out. Gather the community to pray and atone for itself. Sift the grain, get the pebbles out.

Pound the flour, make it fine. Lovingly discipline the children, learn them their boundaries. Pound the flour, discipline the children, make them fine.

Now roast the nuts, warm them over. Gather as family around the fire, warm yourselves over. Roast the nuts, gather around the fire, warm it all over.

Preserve the fruits, dry them and store them in gourds. Tend to and appreciate the elders, seek their wisdom while they have breath to tell it. Preserve the fruits, appreciate the elders, prepare for the future.

Salt the greens, let them take on flavor. Let creativity flow in the compound, encourage children and elderly to co-create and give stage to divinity. Salt the greens, let creativity flow in the compound, give stage to divinity.

Rinse Earth off the squash, let their colors out. Keep clean the compound, roads, homes and gathering places. Have pride in your appearance as a people. Rinse Earth off the squash, cleanse the compound, take pride.

Boil the sweet potato, soften its amber flesh. Practice proper herbal medicine so that the place where children grow and roam is sterile and goodness flows. Boil the sweet potato, soften its amber flesh.

Ripen the plantain, bring it to proper sweetness. Bring the children through their rites of passage, from birth to passing, so that people may be in rhythm with their proper place. Ripen the plantain, ripen the children, create the proper rhythm in their proper place.

Butter the yams, give them honey glow. Mend ruptures between man and woman, soul and soul, parent and child, that there may be continuity of flow, and that the web of Life may go unbroken in mind. Butter the yams, give relationships a honey glow.

Whip the milk to butter, make a food for richening. Work communally to bring wealth to each family, so that pools of finance, and medicine, and learning, and spirit brim over with abundance. Whip the milk to butter, make the compound a wealthy place.

Cool the cream, make it digestible and soothing. Let the people practice their faith and create a blanket of peace, patience and tolerance within their space. That no foreign energy may bring negativity or pre-judgment to a place where there is but one judge Most High. Cool the cream, let there be peace.

Let the children help the mothers gather onions, celery, parsley, basil and cloves. Let grandfathers work with the fathers to prepare the wheat and draw the palm oil from the trees. Let daughters show brothers how to pull leaves from the cabbage. Let sons help sisters carry melons, avocados and tomatoes to grandmothers for slicing.

Let whole families clean the conch shells that grown folks have gathered from the seas. Let the tallest children pick the highest hanging bananas and mangos and pass them to the shortest for basketing. Let them all carry those baskets back to the compound.

Let, finally, every person, no matter how wealthy or needy, no matter how young or old, how able or disabled, how respected or stigmatized, how blessed with family or without, how learned or unknowing, how spiritual or religious, how powerful or powerless, let every human person share in the blessing of what the Earth and Creator have provided.

And let this feasting be done socially in recognition of the oneness of Life, so that a magical, spiritual transformation may take place: Each person eating of Life itself, relating to each other person no matter how different or disliked, because that person is eating of Life itself. All present drinking the sustenance of fluid, which flows through us and between us as does the Spirit.

A human feast, with humans at their most human, recognizing fulfillment in themselves and each other, parents thankfully tearful for the provision of food for their children, children blissfully unconcerned with painful things as they fill warmly their bellies, elderly, eyes glistening with pride and acceptance as they behold the generations that they have unleashed. A great cycle continued, with seven generations before sitting present at the feast and saying: *We have taught you well.* And seven generations yet to come also sitting present and saying: *We hope you teach us so well.*

Life is going down throats into bellies. Spirit is quenching thirst and dripping from chins. The community is alive. In togetherness. All is well.

*December 9, 1997

BLACK WRINKLES

I give thanks to my Black Elders
when I see them on the street.

I give thanks because they walked
a rougher path before me,
beating down the stones,
leveling the terrain,
enduring the impossible
pain.

Now, I walk on smoother ground
Because of their blood and tears...
scars and fears,
but beyond that,
because of their strength
and depth and resilient breath.

So, yes,
I appreciate, I cherish
my Black Elders,
and for this
I give them deference.

I kiss Black Grandmothers
because I know what they have done.

Their life-marked lips
have kissed the stars
and moved the sun.
I know what they have done.

I smile at the sight of soulful elderly
because in my mind
Black Wrinkles are a badge
of victory,
of life sustained,
of wisdom ingrained,
of tribulation's glory rain,
of the burdened living
through days that come after
death of sons and daughters,
and grandchildren too,
of the tears that have soaked
tracks of wrinkle
in leathered skin,
filling in the trenches
like warm water come again
along the groove of a dried-out
river bed,

of the pain they have bled.

I long to touch just a fingertip
to each memory reflected
in their clouded eyes
and say in truth,

I have recognized the stories
within your eyes,
and I shall carry them here,
in my tender heart,
to the next generation.

What you have known
will be repeatedly known again,
to my progeny,
to their offspring,
to the seventh generation of kin.

And in the comfort of this transaction,
my Black Elders might finally grasp
a certain kind of peace,
knowing that their storied-eyes
need no longer stay awake,
that they may pass to another place,
to another garden
and gain again
that youthful sprout,
starting over in a next cycle,
to breathe,
to gather a new collection of stories within
nostalgic eyes.

The noose, the shackle,
the baying hound,
the scalding sting
of an August cotton ground,

the whip, the black law baton,
the robe of justice in gaveled frown,
the humiliation, the scorn,
the trading block,
lips pulled back like with a horse
to reveal tender gums
and the rotted beat of scurvy drums,

nightmares of husbands lost,
criminal sex and seminal frost,
frigid gives what frigid takes,
the frostbitten lives
of previous Black souls
perishing in slavery lakes.

Bones stuck
with Mastodon repose
in tar-like swamps,
lending evidence of a tortured time,
a museum for the modern mind,
but never, ever,
the raw, bleeding truth
that once brought warm water
rampaging from slavery lakes
through river beds,
never, this,

pause for effect...

absolute understanding
that experience brings.

And so I bow to my Black Elders
...in prayer for freedom rings.

One day I shall kiss
that crowning jewel,
that ring of honor
upon time-twisted hands,
and in my nighttime I shall dream
of warm water turned

to refreshing cool,
retreating back up the divides
of salted skin,
and I will smile in cadence
with cricket songs.

Dawn draws nigh,
Emergent... the sun,
moved a full hand's distance
across the sky...

My God,
Black Elder,
please stand still,
draw a deeper breath,
and kindly let me look...

There.

...words escape.

One comes.

Bend close,
let me whisper...

*June 1, 1995

NACALA

The sound is…

Nacala

a single blade of jade grass
rises in the gathering place

a silent summoning
comes forth from
this tender uprising

all things living
sense this stirring
this single blade of jade
this insurgent sable
this edged ebony
oblique obsidian

rising in the gathering place

they come
they gather
for she who was born
five thousand moons ago
inside an African heart
that beat
inside an African chest
that walked African earth
breathed African air

born five thousand moons ago
beside a bold lagoon
beneath a revival of falcons
to the song of river cane waking

born with a notion too strong
for gentle calligraphy
and so set in proud script

born with a volcanic knowing
catching the cold taste of
injustice on the tongue
spitting that tang into the dust

determined to see fruit ripen
destined to reach the high branches

your song saying:

if I rise
I will see
a most glorious thing

if I believe
I will make mountains
emerge from mist

if I choose
herds will stampede
the tainted towers

if I speak
Creation will turn Its ears

If I rise

separated
for five thousand moons
from your song
though still it resides
in your marrow
sleeping
stirring
mumbling
moving you

and now this season
of becoming
this thirteen sun circles
this woman movement
yam dancing in earth
plantain pulsing
night owl circum-seeing

something solid
breaking through the crust

and you must
you must remember
Nacala

remember your song
remember the notes
you taught us then

to sing you now

see Sankofa bird
beyond your circumstance
it caws a kind of memory

reach up and reclaim
your life's true code
from its hopeful feathers

remember
a circle around you
and distant elders
pouring their hopes into you

remember the strong brew
that made the whole tribe drunk
that strong brew was you

remember the teachings
the old one by the stump
poured over you

in sap and song
she bathed you
in what it means to be woman
what it means to walk as woman
speak as woman
hold your body as woman

she whispered the secret
into you *Nacala*

she whispered:

speak with a graceful tongue

she whispered:

do no harm to you
do not harm to others
do no harm

she showed you
the artifacts of Greatness
stowed in the treasure chest
of an old tree trunk

the pearl of Compassion
the branch of Oneness
the raindrop of Honor
the sun shaft of Love

in secrecy she handed you these
—your life's endowments

she showed you
the polished mirror
of obsidian

you looked in
you saw you

you saw you
you Black bamboo
born green and unknowing

rising swiftly into sky
gaining height
gaining vision

turning to ebony
not in skin
in character
absorbing the qualities
of gorgeous dark dignity
claiming the blanket
of Indigenous humility
the way night does not
brag or whistle
but just draws its wide cloak
over day and dominates

you single blade of jade
turning into night
turning into your womanhood

remember what it means
to be *Greatness*

reign in your power to destroy
cast the net of your Creator power
cast it over our depleted waters
pull up schools of vision
and feed us your dreams
feed us your fire

remember your sister Sojourner
and your twin Harriet
go find them and bring them

to us

throw a rebellion
beneath the canopy
of calloused hearts

burn down our fickle forest
construct a new community

do it with your gifts
Nacala

your tongue of Grace
your vision sublime
your mystical seeing
your trenchant song

do it with your gifts
you singular blade of jade
you enormous instrument
of heart looking for its heart
Love looking for its design

all things living
come now to this
gathering place
which is you

we look to you

remember when you were born
those five thousand moons ago?

we stood around you in circle
and said among ourselves:

look at this one
look at this unimaginable drum

we look to you

polish your ebony soul
resurrect your Light-nature
this is the age you meet two roads
one runs to ruin
the other is a trail of Peace

choose your life
you grand canyon performing
you disobedient parting of sea

choose your life of stupendous magma
and eruption into sky

calm your false fissures
seal your seductive cracks
remember yourself

you knew once
so many moons ago
how to walk through this world
touching everything
harming nothing
lifting oceans and peaks
with your inspired genius

now is the season of your
rebirth

be born again
and remember
the you who walks
through worlds
consumed with one
unending mantra:

If I rise...

choose your life
go forward into Grace
shed your old skins
you are the gathering place
we have been waiting for

remember you.

*For Saige Ayan Shoshana Nacala.

*November 21, 2010

FATHER TO SON II

Come here, boy,
sit down for a minute,
I gotta rap something at you.
Nah, nah, this'll just take a minute.

Look at you,
birthday comin' up,
what're you turnin, fifteen?
You think you're a man now, don't you?
You think you ready to take me?
I'm just playin',
but, hey, don't think I don't see that
bloodshot in your eyes,
you think you're ol' man was born yesterday?
I know something about that weed
you obviously been smokin'
Nah... don't even try it,
you don't play me,
I play you,
in this house I'm the player president,
you the butler, Son,

Now look,
I seen you trippin down that brown muddy
river
you call being grown skippin stones
from the safety of your
sheltered youth
across the water
at so called enemies
you call 'em enemies

those rituals and symbols
you adorn your language with:

the brothers from the other
side of the city,
the punks who looked wrong at you
or who stepped on your shoes,
all the fools who disrespected you,
Society, authority, the Man,
the system, supremacy,
Yeah, I see who you skip your
flat stones at:

everybody got it in for you, right?

The water's so smooth
you can't hardly wait
to skip that stone
skip it skip it
Your Momma's milk
still droppin from your lip
but you can't wait to skinny dip
get naked and wade out in that water
so you can reach the other side
with your skippin stones

but check this, Young,
your male masquerade
racial righteousness
Afrocelebratory rage
needs to catch some recognition
of its contradiction

You call yourself strong Black African
representing the Spiritual?
When you reduce all this
human madness down to its core
when you percolate the coffee black down to
its juice
one truth flows loose
Spirit don't respect nobody
who can't respect it back
The whole point of Spirit
is to be recognized
in everything

You think you're deep
by espousing some sort of
Black loyalty?
You're missing the point,
the challenge,
the purpose of being here
on this Earth.

The point of pain
is to challenge us to retain
the ability to recognize Spirit
where it becomes most painful
to see it,
nothing more nothing less.

The more pain a people are given
from Above,
the more purpose those people
have to transform themselves,
like coal through pressure to diamond,

from crushed humanity to risen regality,
not poisoned profanity,

the point of pain is not to stop
believing in the value of Love,
but to gain a more productive understanding
of what Love is.

It's a shame,
you actually have to defend
Loving people these days.

Don't you let anyone tell you
Love is soft.
Prejudice and dehumanization
are soft
Love is hard,
it's the hardest thing there is.

Love isn't the kisses and hugs,
it's the pain of respecting the life force
of a fool you disagree with,
it's not the romance,
it's the surrender of ego when
your Loved one needs you
to just be there for them,

it's not passivity, blindness,
or allowing someone to injure you,
it's the ability to acknowledge
your own imperfection
in relation to someone
you are motivated to judge as flawed,

it's not about puffing out your chest
on the street or schoolyard,
it's about holding in the harmful stuff
you wish to spit out
at someone who has hurt you,

it's not about passing on lessons
to your children
about how you don't like this
or that group of people,
but struggling to teach
that at the bottom of the well
and the end of the day
there must reverence for something
which is greater
than our human drama,
and that thing is Life which is Spirit,
which is thunder to our whisper,
is typhoon to our tear,
is the matter which composes us
and allows us the opportunity
to breathe in the first place.

Love is a lonely, painful, bleeding, frustrating,
drum beat to commit to
on an Earth where we cower
behind false fronts
of false strength and false wisdom,

but know that to the degree
you achieve this thing,
Love,
that is the degree to which you

have fulfilled your purpose
and prepared a path with full paving
for the next seven generations
to play and work and build upon.

Love may leave you feeling naked,
but Son, you need to feel naked sometimes,
and if the wind jump up and bite you, then
you take your licking and go on,
but if you bundle up constantly
to avoid the cold,
you will live your life in hiding
from the very Sun
which makes you a living,
breathing thing.

All y'all young'ns are scared to death
of Lovin somebody,
especially yourselves.

You call that being hard
being strong
being true soldiers,
Man, put away those toy guns
and those kiddy costumes
and sign up for the real battle.

A people don't rise up by hating
'cause hate is a self-destroyer,

a people don't rise by dehumanizing
psychologies,
because those are only self-destroyers,

a people don't rise by building
paradigms of superiority,
that's cowardice that comes from
the ones who did it to them
in the first place,

Our poet queen talkin about *still I rise,*
it's Spirit she's talking about,
and Spirit doesn't have the ego
and fears necessary to care a drop
about which people started what
and whose culture is cause for
laying down the carpet of prejudice
so a fearful group can walk
over bodies
to some supposed glory land.

Black Moses didn't need
that kind of a helping hand,
Tubman didn't take the time
to feed her prejudices
toward the people
who caused her pain,
she just knew she had to
get her people up out
from under the whip,
cause the whip was causing
rivers of raised skin to sprout out
all over her people's backs,
she knew the tracks,
she didn't look back.

Y'all think strappin down with a piece
will bring you peace,
and y'all end up doin nothin
but restin in peace,

that safety release,
that bad boy's the beast,
you got glocs taped in your socks,
thinking you's a man,
you wanna know about a man?

This here's your grandfather,
Boss here lived through mess
that would have you
shakin in your shoes,
drownin in your bad news,
but didn't do much more to him
than make him pull up on the porch
and sing him some blues,
lived through hell year after year
for one hundred and four,
raised five boys on his own
in a shack in the woods,
livin on grits from dawn
to dusk,

this man split open his palms
each day on the thorns
and bark and cotton
and stones of the earth
and you know who he was
livin for?
he was living for you, Son.

See when you have a reason,
then you do what it takes,
y'all just give up too easy now,
you don't realize you got people
not yet born depending on you.

Some folk call a baby born dead
still born 'cause the baby ain't moving,
my daddy's people
don't see it that way,
they say a baby born dead
is moving plenty,
its spirit is moving quick
on to the next place,
it's only the the body
that ain't movin,
they still call it a still born though,
my Daddy's people,
'cause even though that baby
doesn't seem to have
a living purpose
for being in this world
it's still born,
still born,
see, that's a recognition of purpose,

those babies are born because
they are part of an experience that
goes beyond them as individuals,

in the brief flash of their presence here,
they affect the growth and path-walking of
the people closest to them,

who in turn affect the generations
ahead, partly because of what
they experienced in that
short time with that majestic spirit housed in
the humble, helpless body
of a newborn
still born,

all that heartbreak
and yet still born

you got to be still born, Son,
it don't matter if your teachers
don't believe in you,
that you can't get that heart-breakin
Lover out of your head,
it don't matter how easy it is
to yank on that weed all day
and float above your troubles,
or how much it hurts
to come crashin back down
when the high is gone
and have them troubles still be there,

it don't matter how much
it splits open your heart each night
when the distractions are gone and nothin's
left but the truth,
the truth that your dear Momma's
gone too,
it don't matter, Son,
you got to be still born,

even with all that Life's handed you,
you were still born,
you got a purpose,
something you're supposed
to rise above, recover from,

but you wouldn't know that,
would you, 'cause you have not yet
learned the value of history, have you?
All you know about is Columbus
and Pilgrims and dead presidents
who spill out of the pages
of your mainstream textbooks,

you don't know nothing
about the truth researched in fire
and written in tears
by John Hope Franklin
and John Henrik Clarke
and Ivan Van Sertima,
do you?

Why you think they spilled blood
out from all them books for?
they was letting the past come howling
through the graveyard
to smack us upside the head
and let us know there's a reason
the dead are dead,

those souls passed on
are the pages we're supposed to turn

to educate ourselves toward our
emancipation,

You think Lincoln
or any other man in a suit
has the power to emancipate?
only a people leaving the pages
of the departed stained
with dirty prints from studious hands,
and who bathe in the water
of ancestral, oral history
have the capacity to unshackle themselves
from that which
binds them,

you got to get to know these people,
Son,
you aren't the first,
your ideas aren't the original,
there aren't any new discoveries
on this Earth,
only fools think that,
fools who have the arrogance to think they
were the first ones
to find the egg
when not only have others
already found the egg,
but they've eaten, digested
and excreted the egg,
then fertilized the ground
with that egg,
grown crops up off that soil,
fed chickens with the grain

from those crops,
and had those chickens
drop more eggs,
the same eggs
these fools like Columbus
are beating their chests
for so called discovering,

so when you go around
talkin' about being grown,
just know you ain't quite ready
for the throne,
when you call yourself being a man,
realize it takes a lot of humbling
to become a man,

are you ready yet
to take the macho off your chest?

And, Son,
now, now... listen to me on this,
ask yourself, Son,
what kind of Love relationship
do you want, if you want one at all,
cause the world inside you that
you allow and heal and grow,
and the world inside your Lover
that they determine,
that will be your relationship.

Y'all will be spending time with
each other's soul, history,
memory, ways, and energy,

and that time will by far
eclipse your experience
with their body and face.
Goodness, please,
learn this Grace.

I'd like to talk to you
about assassins, Son,

assassins cut down
El Hajj Malik El-Shabazz,
Martin, Biko, Medgar too,
back to all the revolutionaries
who took fire to the thin skin
of oppression,
go back to Christ and see,
when the status quo get to
being terrified their terrible time
is up, I promise you they'll come
for the ones who won't bend down,
shuffle up, surrender
their sovereign soul,

If you cause fear
In the supremacy caste,
Negro, you got to go,

row after row of lynched up
Negro,
somebody paint a blood mural
in this piss yellow
supremacy snow.

Son, you got to understand,
there's always gonna be
somebody out there
trying to cut you down,

that don't mean you got to
lie down for 'em,
don't do them that favor,

I don't care what it takes,
educate yourself, study yourself,
prepare yourself to succeed,
but wait a minute,
I've gone on a tangent,

I'm gonna talk with you
about something I know...
Son, if you ever have the sacred
honor of placing your two hands
on the bare full hips of a woman,
kill all commotion
and listen for her inside ocean,
get still, and your hands will fill
with a silent vibration,

that space from pelvis bone
to pelvis bone
composes the throne
on which the first sunrise shone,
so if ever you're all a-moan
about the drama you believe
your woman is puttin you through,
put your two hands on

her bare full hips
and imagine all the drama that
through the ages
have come through her
from all those male dictators
sitting falsely on her throne,
and then just you try and moan.

And, Son, we got to do something
About all these fights
you keep getting caught up in,

now, I'm glad you know how
to put a whuppin on somebody,
but come on now, Son,
everybody in the whole world
can't be your enemy.

What do you mean you can't
let them think you're soft?
That you're trying to be
a true soldier?
Boy...

Let me tell you something,
carrying Love in your heart
doesn't mean you trust others
blindly,
it means you find the courage
and reason to keep open your
heart and keep unpolluted your
soul, through painful work in
the dirt of your ego and pride,

because you know
the act of spirituality
is the act of Love,
is the recognition and practice
of Creation's oneness
even if it hurts,
especially if it hurts,
for humility is an elusive garden,
but to let it die is a certain death,

and it doesn't mean you let people trespass
against your soul,
it means in your reaction
to their trespass
you find the dignity
to retain a reverence
for the Spirit of life
within them,

it doesn't mean you accept
a genocidal movement
against your people,
it means that in your resistance
and revolution against destruction
you carry yourself as a true soldier,

all this talk
about being an African warrior...
true warriors back in the day
were brave and wise enough
to revere and honor the
Life Spirit of their so called *enemy*,
even if they were willing to die

fighting that enemy,

A true warrior knew an enemy
was defined not by tribal affiliations
or life stations,
but by what was beating
in the breast of that soul
when they stood close enough
to smell each other's deepest truth bubbling
up on the crest
of each other's sweat,

a true warrior
had the courage to use prejudice
and dehumanizing reasoning
only as desperate last resorts,
and did not walk so quickly
toward those last resorts,
because the warrior knew
once arrived at that place
of regarding the enemy
as less than human,
that in that spiritual moment
of raged engagement,
the warrior would become
less than human, too,

the true warrior
knew all this because
the elders told so,
told so repeatedly from the time
of the warrior's childhood,
to the coming of age ceremony,

that one should never
look for the enemy
by the appearance
of the physical body,
that the true warrior
must endure the pain
of uncertainty
and seek the enemy
in a more hidden place,
the heart,

true warriors,
contrary to our notions
of masculine strength,
shed countless nighttime tears
through childhood years
as they bit their lips
to bear the pain of uncertainty
in reserving judgement of another,
then they wiped that copper-tasting blood
from lip wound
and spread it over
their salted eyes
so they could attain the vision
of one who finds the enemy
in its true nest,
the beating heart,
the polluted river of spirit,

the elders told this,
that all the pain a people
might be given to suffer
over the course of generations

would not be a test
of how angry or hateful
or vengeful or fearful
a people could grow,
but would be a test
of how much blindness
for seeing heart and spirit
they could resist,

those people, it was told,
who succumbed to fear and pain
by looking for the enemy
in the physical appearance
of another,
soon found their own camp
consumed in fires of spite,
for the enemy,
unseen by the spiritually blind,
crept into the hearts
of such person's own family,
friends, and community,
and became them,

the enemy became them,

the elders have always known
that the enemy of humankind
is not a physical, genetic force,
but a foul wind that blows
through the doors left open
by fearful hearts,
a wind which respects
no genetic boundaries

or cultural self-satisfactions,
a poisoned wind which feasts
on those who confuse
cultural celebration
with the salivations of superiority,

and for all those who claim
African righteousness
as they walk with prejudiced hearts,
they should know that it is an
African tale which tells that:

If you are a jackal and decide
that the hyena is the enemy,
when you next turn around
all the hyenas will be wearing
jackal skins,
and you won't know if you're
about to be fed or killed
when your own momma grins,

the noose never loosens
if you use it, so lose it,
lose the narrow minded tactics,
life isn't only in the didactics,
most folks come as partial exceptions
to all our social rules and rumors,
no catalogued reference point
will cover something as vast
as a life created by a
supreme creator
who shakes Its head in dismay
while we march pathetically

on prejudice campaigns
toward our decay,
slicin and dicin folks
on the basis of labels,
longest running show on earth,
we Cains slayin Abels,

Son, you gotta understand
that to live with true peace
in your heart is the hardest,
most painful way of living
for we who have been made
to bleed across generations
and continents,
but it is also the only reason
we have been here on this journey
in the first place,
to withstand the pain
and still rise, a spiritual people,
a soul-land
where Love still lives.

all that pain,
generation after generation,
and still born,
still born to rise
and be beautiful enough
to truly, sacredly, soulfully live.

I'm not concerned about
no melting pots,
cultural conflict is and always
will be an aspect of humanity,

I'm not in Love with the idea
of groups coming together
under the terms of oppression,
showing more loyalty to
conformity within a status quo
than to freedom and the
medicine seeds it sows,

I am in Love
with the Spirit of Life
that flows through souls,
and am bound by my faith
to die if necessary to beget
that Spirit unleashed on Earth.

I never wanted you to make
every person your friend,
you ain't even got time
or reason for that,
I just want you to stop
being so afraid to recognize
that somebody is human
with all the uniqueness
and capacity to grow
that you have,

Son, when your Momma was sick
and moving on from here,
she wrote you a letter and made me
promise to give it to you
when you were ready,
so here it is:

My Dear Love,

These days
I seem to be more in the next world
than in this one,
it feels as though my body
is being spread out
like crumbs on the beach
for the seagulls to pick up
and scatter out to sea,
but I feel good about that, my child,
I know this is my place on the road,
and my thoughts now
are mostly with you,

when you come of age
to read these words,
I imagine you'll be dealing with your father's
long-winded father-son "*conversations*"
and I want you to know something...

I think I can best say it like this...

It's hard to express
the depth of something
like a Love for your child,
but maybe you can understand
if I tell you that many nights
after he had read you to sleep,
your father would come to bed
and put his head on my shoulder,

he would begin to tell stories
about how you remind him of when
he was young, you know,
back when Run DMC
was the place to be,
and how he would get up early
before anyone else to watch
the cartoons and eat from his stash
of candy he hid in his pillow case,
and how the morning sun
coming in from the window would massage
his skin back to warm
while he drank his personal
concoction of hot chocolate,
cause he hated drinking that milk
his Momma always watered down
to make it last longer,

Your father would tell these stories
most nights, and at some point along
the way, I could feel wetness pool
on my shoulder,
and I knew he was crying,

I believe he was crying
tears of happiness
because he knew
the child's excitement
that must be coursing through you
like it did then through him,

you see, my child,
you were your father's memories,
his reflection pond,
and daily he interrupted his own flow
to come beside you,
and gaze into his yesterdays,

I want you to know this because
I imagine growing into a man
will be a struggle for you
like it is for most,
and I want you to remember
on those stone hard days when
the pain is greater than advertised,
and it seems you've lost your way
and can't find yourself,
remember that your life has meaning
and value and promise,
and that someone very beautiful,
your father,
is finding himself in you,

I don't fear for you
because you are Black,
my son,
I fear for you because
the rest of the world isn't,
and something hostile
comes with that truth,

but I do also know
there is a purpose for your life,
and that one day,

despite all the pain,
your personhood, your ability
to live in the succulence
of your intrinsic beauty,
will still be born,

and I will be with you,
in every bit of sky you breathe
and each spark of sunlight
touching your
precious
precious
skin.

*February 25, 1999

NOTE FROM THE PUBLISHER

Father to Son is a spoken word song and prayer. Much of its power, richness, and nuance can be experienced uniquely in audio form. Besides Jaiya's own recordings of this work, we hope you will encourage and create spaces for young people in particular to share this message in their voice and spirit.

We also encourage you to introduce *Father to Son* as a book resource for young people, families, parents, caregivers, leaders, youth programs, agencies, schools, libraries, and community initiatives in your area.

Among many social issues, *Father to Son* addresses the following:

- Parenting
- Fatherhood
- Womanhood
- Family and Community
- Love Relationships
- Education and Empowerment
- History, Heritage, and Ancestry
- Positive Identity and Self-Love
- Leadership and Role Modeling
- Spirituality and Sacredness
- Healing from Trauma
- Anger and Violence

- Racism, Stigma, and Prejudice
- Purpose and Giftedness
- The Power of Creativity
- Dehumanization
- Oppression
- Rehumanization
- Resilience
- Holistic Wellbeing
- Rites of Passage

We at Soul Water Rising appreciate your sincere support as we continue the freedom work of nurturing the healing and sacred wholeness of our children, families, and communities.

If this book touched you, you can touch it back.

Please consider writing an **online reader review** at Amazon, Barnes & Noble, or Goodreads. Reviews are a valuable way to support the life of a book and especially to support an independent author.

Freely **post social media photos** of you or others with the book, just the book itself, or passages from the book. Please kindly include the hashtag **#JAIYAJOHN.**

I cherish your support of my books and our Soul Water Rising rehumanizing mission around the world.

BOOK ANGEL PROJECT

Your book purchases support our global *Book Angel Project,* which provides scholarships and book donations for vulnerable youth, and places gift copies of my inspirational books throughout communities worldwide, to be discovered by the souls who need them. The books are left in places where hearts are tender: hospitals, nursing homes, prisons, wellness centers, group homes, mental health clinics, and other community spaces.

If you are fortunate to discover one of our *Book Angel* gift books, please kindly post a photo of the book on Instagram, using the hashtag **#JAIYAJOHN**, or email it to us at **books@soulwater.org**. Thank you!

I Will Read for You:
The Voice and Writings of Jaiya John

Dr. Jaiya John shares freedom work and healing messages with audiences worldwide. He was orphan-born on Ancient Puebloan lands in the desert of New Mexico, is a former professor of social psychology at Howard University, and has lived in various locations, including Kathmandu, Nepal. Jaiya is the author of numerous books, and the founder of Soul Water Rising, a global rehumanizing mission supporting the healing and wholeness of vulnerable and historically oppressed populations.

Jacqueline V. Carter and Kent W. Mortensen served graciously, faithfully, and skillfully as editors for *Freedom*. I am forever grateful for their Love labor.

Secure a Jaiya John reading, keynote, or talk:

jaiyajohn.com

OTHER BOOKS BY JAIYA JOHN

Jaiya John titles are available online where books are sold. To learn more about this and other books by Jaiya, to order **discounted bulk quantities**, and to learn about Soul Water Rising's global freedom work, please visit us at:

jaiyajohn.com

books@soulwater.org

@jaiyajohn (IG FB TW YT)

USE THIS SPACE FOR YOUR NOTES

USE THIS SPACE FOR YOUR NOTES

www.ingramcontent.com/pod-product-compliance
Lightning Source LLC
Chambersburg PA
CBHW030818190426
43197CB00036B/590
* 9 7 8 0 9 9 1 6 4 0 1 4 0 *